CW00919533

ANGELS CAME CALLING

MESSAGES FROM HEAVEN

L P FARRELL

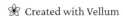 Created with Vellum

FOREWORD

For my Father.

I know you're at peace now and you're watching over me from above. This is my gift to you, coming a heart that is filled with so much love. I miss you more and more each day. Xxx

1

MESSAGES FROM HEAVEN

———

I did not want to leave you, I asked if I could stay. Then I felt a peaceful light wash over me and it took my fears away.

2

MESSAGES FROM HEAVEN

———

I whispered goodbye when the angels came and told me it was time. I kissed you softly and held your hand and comforted you as you cried.

3
MESSAGES FROM HEAVEN

———

When I feel your pain takeover and see your sorrow grow, I surround you with my angelic love and help your sadness go.

4

MESSAGES FROM HEAVEN

———

When you are overwhelmed with sorrow and feel like a lonesome dove, I'll whisper to you softly, watching over you from above.

5
MESSAGES FROM HEAVEN

———

I watched you cry as you said goodbye, I was sitting by your side. Please know that I was with you and that I too cried.

6

MESSAGES FROM HEAVEN

_____

I know your heart is hurting and I cannot be there, but I promise you I'm at peace now and waiting for you here.

7
MESSAGES FROM HEAVEN

———

I'm in a peaceful place now, high up in the sky and that sorrow that you're feeling, I promise will heal in time.

8

MESSAGES FROM HEAVEN

That piece of your heart in heaven with me is kept safely by my side. I feel its love wash over me and I'm filled with so much pride.

9
MESSAGES FROM HEAVEN

———

Those unexpected visits from friends are special gifts from me. I see you struggling with your pain and that's not how I want it to be.

10

MESSAGES FROM HEAVEN

———

Your love is a bright beacon that I can see from far above. I come down to see you always and my heart is filled with love.

11

MESSAGES FROM HEAVEN

———

The pain in your heart in time will heal and I'll be by your side. An unseen presence always with you, I will be your guide.

12

MESSAGES FROM HEAVEN

———

I cannot wait to see you again and share my stories from up high. I know I'll keep you smiling with my tales from the heavenly sky.

13
MESSAGES FROM HEAVEN

———

E ven though I am in heaven now, I miss you every day. I wish you could see me when I come to visit you and I wish that I could stay.

14

MESSAGES FROM HEAVEN

———

I did not want to leave you, it was not my choice to stay, the angels came and called my name and brought me far away.

15
MESSAGES FROM HEAVEN

———

D eath does not break the bond of love, it simply reminds us it was real. We're connected now through a heavenly light that we both will forever feel.

16

MESSAGES FROM HEAVEN

———

Death was so surreal to me, I did not understand, that when that peaceful light washed over me, I'd let go of your hand.

17

MESSAGES FROM HEAVEN

———

Being a spirit is really strange, I keep looking for my clothes. I know you'd laugh if you could see me now, dressed in my white and silky robes.

18

MESSAGES FROM HEAVEN

———

I'll help you heal in your time of grief and guide you on your journey.

I'll send you signs here and there when times get dark and stormy.

19
MESSAGES FROM HEAVEN

When my heart stop beating, I could still hear your cries. Those sounds you made as I closed my eyes are forever in my mind.

I held your hand that day and comforted you while you cried, until your tears stopped falling, I waited by your side.

20

MESSAGES FROM HEAVEN

———

I know my death has broken you, but your life must go on. Look for me in the beauty of things, it is here my love for you will live on.

21

MESSAGES FROM HEAVEN

―――――

I promise dying did not hurt me, I simply closed my eyes. I took one last deep breath inwards and I flew up to the skies.

22

MESSAGES FROM HEAVEN

———

I did not plan to leave you but for my body it was time. My soul departed for heavenly plains, leaving yours behind.

23
MESSAGES FROM HEAVEN

My place is in the skies now and I am no longer there, I ask you to be kind to yourself and promise me you'll take care.

24

MESSAGES FROM HEAVEN

L ook for me when signs appear, they'll let you know I'm near. I'll always send these gifts to you in times of turmoil and fear.

25
MESSAGES FROM HEAVEN

———

When my last breath left me on that faithful day, I wish you could have seen me gain my angel wings as I flew away.

26

MESSAGES FROM HEAVEN

———

K now that I will always love you and death is not the end, it's simply another chapter in our journey, the rest has yet to be penned.

27
MESSAGES FROM HEAVEN

———

My soul is in a peaceful place, surrounded by love and light. I miss you every single day, I'll guide you when the time is right.

28

MESSAGES FROM HEAVEN

———

I heard the sweet words you spoke of me when you laid my body to rest. I gazed down at you from my place in heaven with pride bursting from my chest.

29
MESSAGES FROM HEAVEN

I wrap my wings around you in your time of need. You sometimes know I'm there when you look right at me and your heart rate picks up speed.

30
MESSAGES FROM HEAVEN

———

I am with you now in spirit, our souls forever entwined. Our bond of love will never die as it was written in the skies.

31
MESSAGES FROM HEAVEN

———

I am blessed that we connected and that I walked with you in life.

My soul waits for yours in heaven, I'll guide you with a loving light.

32
MESSAGES FROM HEAVEN

————

P lease forgive me for leaving you in so much pain. I didn't want to go that day but I had angel wings to gain.

33
MESSAGES FROM HEAVEN

I wish that you could see me now, my wings shimmering with light. Each time I come and visit you, I wrap you up real tight.

34
MESSAGES FROM HEAVEN

———

I watch you on the days you struggle with me dying. I am sorry I cannot be there with you, I wish I could stop you from crying.

35
MESSAGES FROM HEAVEN

G od will give you the strength to recover from losing me to death. I will watch over you in the years to come until you take your last breath.

36
MESSAGES FROM HEAVEN

———

Time in heaven, it has no meaning. Stop worrying about me up here and please focus on your healing.

37

MESSAGES FROM HEAVEN

————

Watch out for me in the clouds when you see the beauty there. I will send you colours in the sky, from my angelic place up here.

38
MESSAGES FROM HEAVEN

———

I'm with you when you call my name and you look for signs I'm there.

I'm sorry you cannot hear my answers, but know I'm always near.

39
MESSAGES FROM HEAVEN

———

This grief you feel is a sad chapter in your life story. If you embrace the pain then let it go, I'll help you heal on this journey.

40
MESSAGES FROM HEAVEN

———

I am overwhelmed with love for you as I watch you from above.

My heart is forever bursting, filled with heavenly pride and love.

41

MESSAGES FROM HEAVEN

I loved you for a lifetime and my death does not change a thing.

I'll show my love differently now, in the beauty of small things.

42
MESSAGES FROM HEAVEN

———

Feathers will appear when I wrap you up in my wings, my dear. I will leave them as a gift for you, a small reminder that I miss you too.

43
MESSAGES FROM HEAVEN

———

I watch you smile when you think of me remembering happy times. One day we'll be together again and our souls will light up the skies.

44
MESSAGES FROM HEAVEN

———

When the stars are shining brightly in the winter sky, look up at me from your place down there and I'll twinkle to say hi.

45
MESSAGES FROM HEAVEN

———

I chose a star close by the house for you to gaze upon. I love watching you stare up at me, the love on your face so strong.

I shine brightly down upon you and keep you safe and warm, a guardian angel watching over you in one of my many forms.

46
MESSAGES FROM HEAVEN

———

When I come and visit you, I wish that I could stay. I love sitting beside you and watching tv when you're having a lazy day.

47
MESSAGES FROM HEAVEN

I sometimes am a robin following you around. You always seem to know it's me when you stop and stare spellbound.

48
MESSAGES FROM HEAVEN

These angel wings are heavy, it took time to get used to mine. I know you would have belly laughed if you'd seen my first time flying.

49
MESSAGES FROM HEAVEN

———

S top worrying about me in heaven, I'm having a great time. I'm catching up with loved ones here and listening to bells chime.

50
MESSAGES FROM HEAVEN

L oving you was easy, it was so hard leaving you behind. Our souls will always be connected and we will meet again in time.

51
MESSAGES FROM HEAVEN

———

I've chosen to be a guardian for lost souls on earth below. I get to visit more often now, and always pop in to say hello.

52
MESSAGES FROM HEAVEN

———

When you wake each morning and I am no longer there. Know that I am still with you, you'll feel it in the air.

53
MESSAGES FROM HEAVEN

———

My love will always surround you and I'll forever be by your side, an unseen presence with you, a spirit form that I must hide.

54
MESSAGES FROM HEAVEN

These new wings are itchy and I sometimes forget they're mine.

Things are so much different now but I am doing absolutely fine.

55

MESSAGES FROM HEAVEN

You need to stop worrying about me, I am not alone. I'm surrounded by loved ones here and we talk about you all down below.

56
MESSAGES FROM HEAVEN

———

I am with you when you visit my resting place and see the sorrow on your face. Those tears make me feel so sad and I wish that we could embrace.

Know that this is not the end, I am waiting for you here, your place will be beside me for a rapturous heavenly cheer.

57
MESSAGES FROM HEAVEN

———

Our memories are gift from God to remind us of our love.

They're created for us by a higher power that is sent from the clouds above.

58
MESSAGES FROM HEAVEN

———

I'm a watchful angel now, looking down on you with pride. One day you'll take your place up here and sit directly by my side.

59
MESSAGES FROM HEAVEN

———

I love to watch you cooking and smile when I hear your curse, that the meal you've prepared burnt again and life couldn't get much worse.

60

MESSAGES FROM HEAVEN

———

I wish that you could feel me when I come down to you from above. I promise I try heal you with the purity of my love.

61

MESSAGES FROM HEAVEN

————

When you're out and are having fun, please stop feeling guilty that my time on earth was done.

I know that you loved me and are having a hard time, you smiling though the pain in your heart, gives me relief in mine.

62

MESSAGES FROM HEAVEN

———

L etting go is painful, and not an easy task. I see you sometimes smiling, struggling behind a mask. Time is a great healer and soon you will be fine, the mask that you are wearing now will disappear in time.

63
MESSAGES FROM HEAVEN

———

I 'll give you the strength to get through your pain and help your mind with healing. You must be honest with your emotions to help stop the painful feelings.

64

MESSAGES FROM HEAVEN

———

L ook for me in the night, for you my star is shining bright.

65
MESSAGES FROM HEAVEN

I miss sharing a joke with you and watching your big smile. I'm grateful that I still get to see you from my place up in the sky.

66

MESSAGES FROM HEAVEN

———

K now that I would have stayed and I promise that I did try and stay with you a little while. You see, the angels, they would not sway from the task God gave them to fly me away.

67
MESSAGES FROM HEAVEN

―――――

I know that you are grieving and you miss me every day, but I must let you in on a secret, my heart hurts in a very bad way.

For when I see you crying and in deep despair, I really want to hug you and let you know that I am still there.

68

MESSAGES FROM HEAVEN

I was sitting on that rainbow as you pointed to the sky. I waved down at you hoping you'd see my beautiful wings as I flew upwards really high.

69
MESSAGES FROM HEAVEN

I'm sorry if I never told you, how proud you make me feel. I loved you every day of my life and want you to now try heal.

70
MESSAGES FROM HEAVEN

———

L ove is the only thing that matters when you are grieving for my loss.

My love for you will never die, it's an eternal force.

71
MESSAGES FROM HEAVEN

———

I look down at you from heaven with a sad smile upon my face. I know that you are hurting but you grieve with so much grace.

72
MESSAGES FROM HEAVEN

I whisper to you throughout the day, oh how I wish that you could hear me.

I love you too, I always will and that is how it will forever be.

73
MESSAGES FROM HEAVEN

———

I miss you always and that will never change. Our souls will meet in heaven again and a big hug we will exchange.

74
MESSAGES FROM HEAVEN

———

I wish that you could see me when I dance around the sky. This wonderful place in heaven is my new home way up high.

75
MESSAGES FROM HEAVEN

———

E ven though I miss you, I understand that in time, our souls will reconnect one day and our love will brightly shine.

76
MESSAGES FROM HEAVEN

———

K now that I'll always love you and I miss you everyday. A piece of my heart is still with you now, your guardian angel I will forever stay.

77

"Death must be so beautiful. To lie in the soft brown earth, with grasses waving above one's head, and listen to silence. To have no yesterday, and no tomorrow. To forget time, to forgive life, to be at peace."

- Oscar Wilde

Printed in Great Britain
by Amazon